MONSTER

A POEM BY
JAMIE HOCKING

ILLUSTRATIONS BY JON HOCKING

DEDICATION

To my husband and soulmate, Jon —
Thank you for always chasing me when I run, and for loving me 'even though'.

To my daughters Josie and Jade —
I will always love you unconditionally – even when you let your monsters out.
Especially when you let your monsters out.

ISBN: 978-0-6458156-9-6

There is a monster

inside of me

and that monster

is me

And I've tried

hiding it away

and I've tried

making it   **CLEAN**

and   ~~**CENSORING**~~

and   **SUFFOCATING**

and   **DROWNING**

AND OH DO I
WANT TO SEE IT

FUCKING

BLEED

But no matter

what I've tried

I cannot

eradicate

this monster

because she

IS PART OF ME

And I misread

the signs

when the

INFINITE
ONENESS

showed itself

to me

I had spent

so long

in the dark

that the light

BLINDED ME

And fooled me

into believing

that the light itself

was the gift -

THE AWAKENING

And proof

that I should seek

INFINITE JOY

IN THE ONENESS
OF NON-DUALITY

Without

the wisdom

of knowing

or accepting

that the Infinite Oneness

by definition

must include

ALL THINGS

THE DARKNESS
THE MISERY

THE SUFFERING
THE TRAGEDY

And so

one truth

I have been

missing

is that darkness

and light

and every shade

IN BETWEEN

are all woven together

to make up

you

and me

and everything

And if love

is reserved

for only

WHAT WE EXPOSE
TO THE LIGHT

Then nobody

is given the chance

to know

or to love

THE WHOLENESS
OF ANY BEING

And here

I deny myself

of the TRUTH

which I claim

to always

be seeking

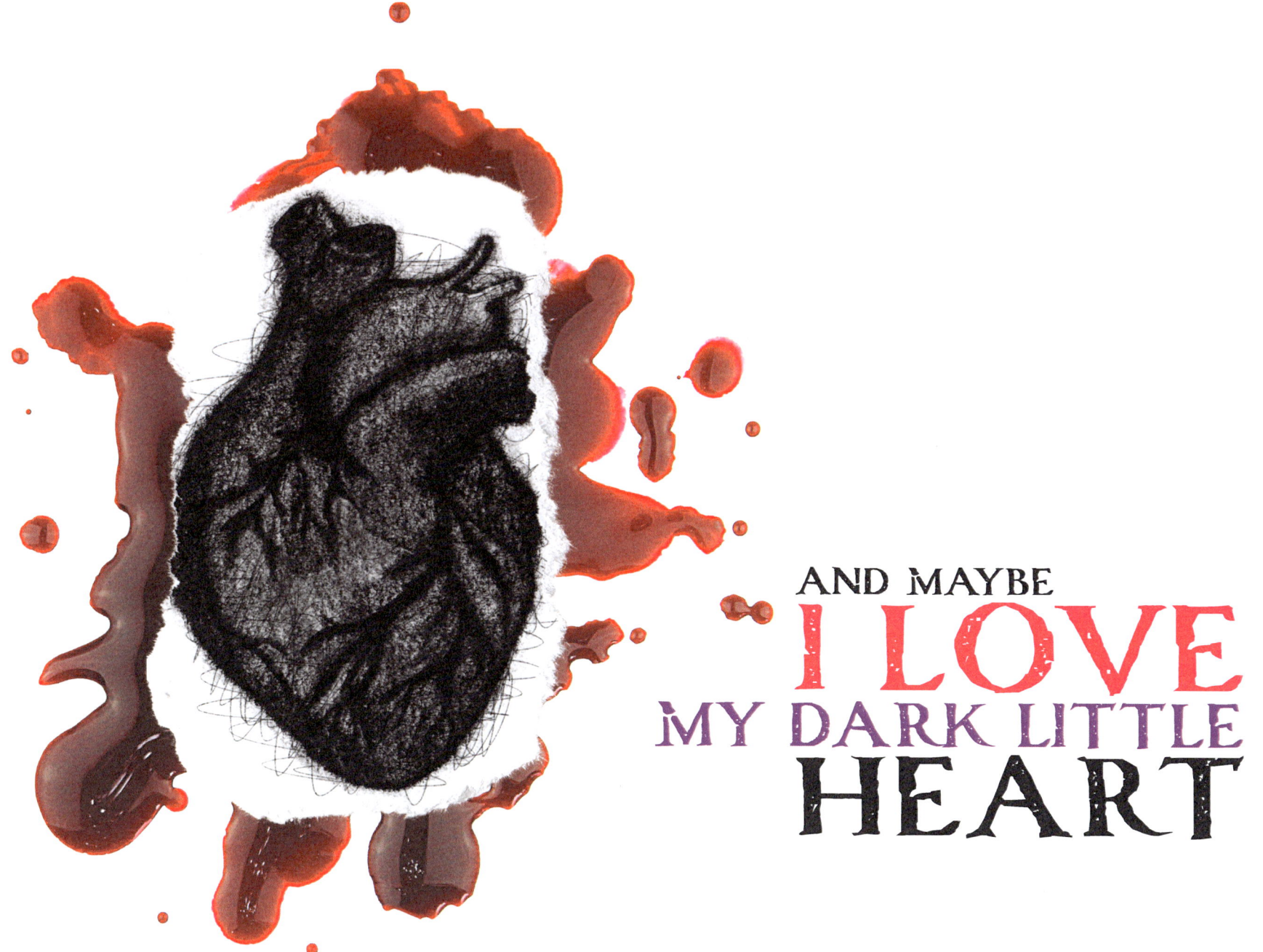

AND MAYBE
I LOVE
MY DARK LITTLE
HEART

and my

DEPTH

The darkness
the misery
the suffering
the tragedy
in the
light

and my

MYSTERY

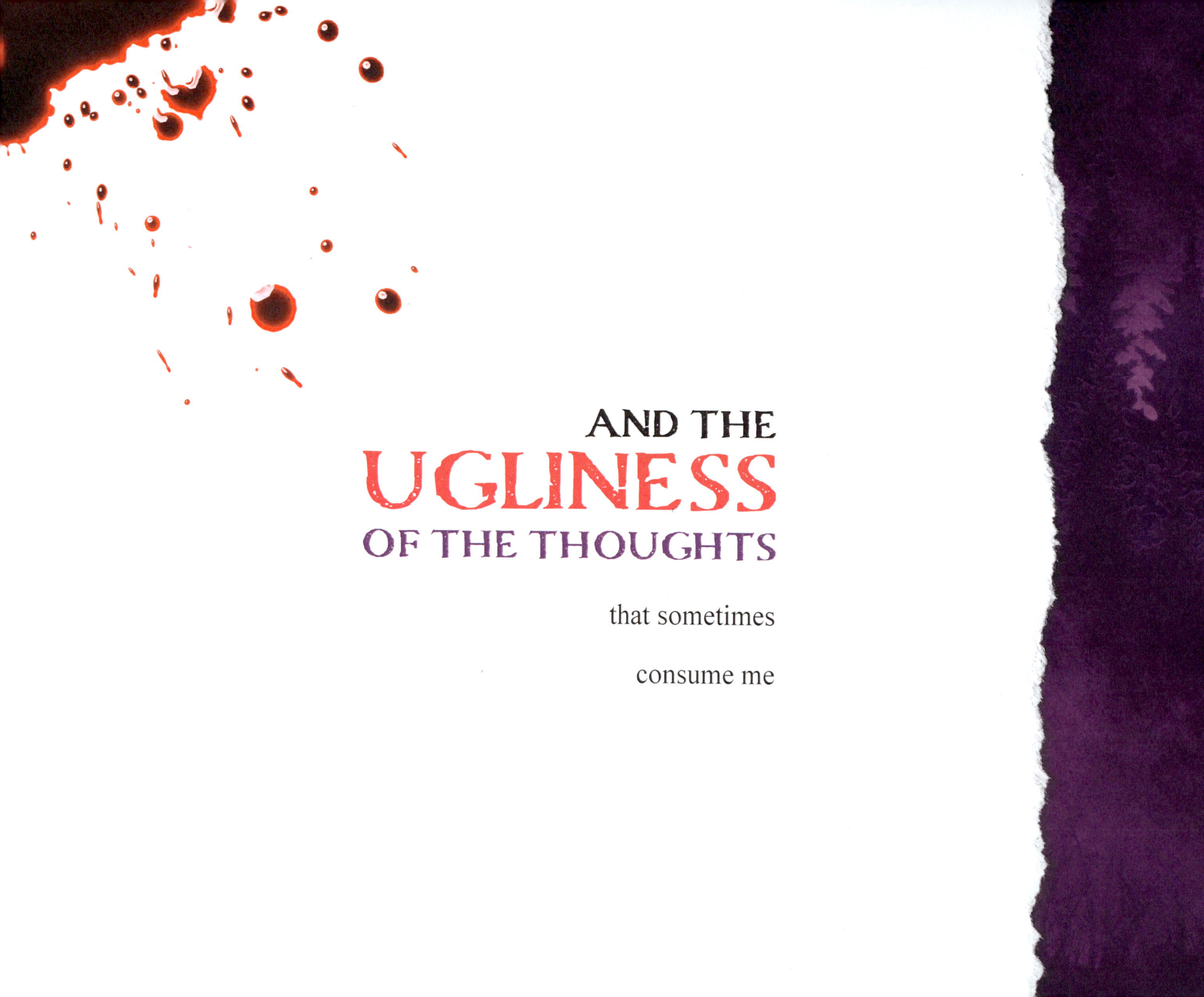

AND THE
UGLINESS
OF THE THOUGHTS

that sometimes

consume me

And the parts

of me

that don't bother

**TAKING IT ALL
SO SERIOUSLY**

AND THE PARTS OF ME
THAT DRIP
WITH WICKEDNESS
AND WITH THE SHAME
OF SINNING

and the ANGER

and the RAGE

and the WARRIOR

and the FREAK

Pretending

provides

no shelter or

ANY

LASTING

PEACE

So why not

become

EVERY

ITERATION

OF ME?

Why not

interrupt

the

REGULARLY
SCHEDULED
PROGRAMMING?

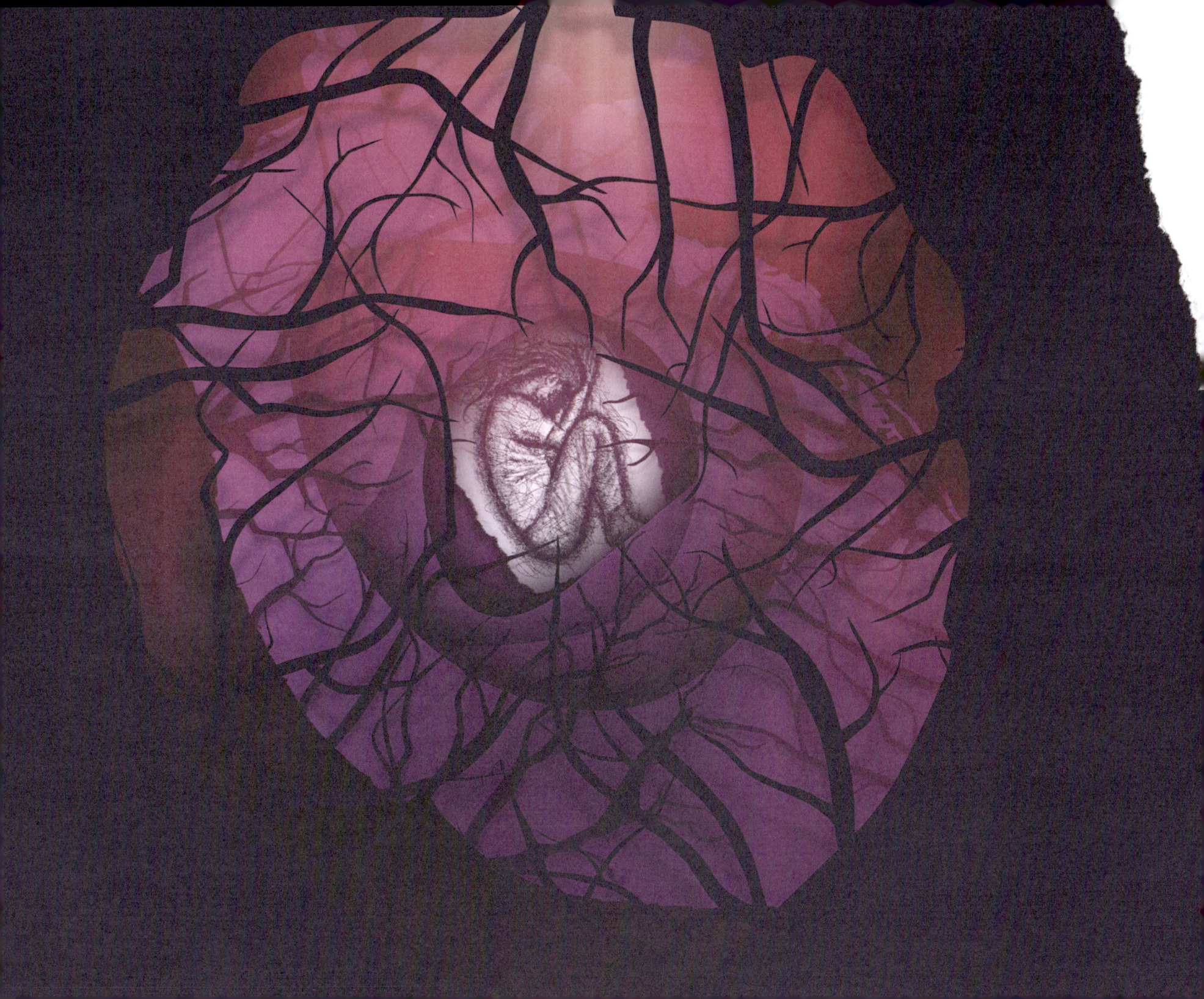

Why not

take my foot

off the throat

of the monster

AND LET IT
BREATHE

and SPEAK
and STOMP
and SCREAM

And make

all the

NOISE

I'VE HELD

INSIDE OF ME?

Why not?

WHY THE FUCK NOT?

Indeed!

THANK YOU

I'd like to thank the people who have extended love, compassion, and acceptance to me – even when they've seen the monsters in me. Without you I would not have been able to let my monsters out, and I would not have come as far as I have in my healing – or in sharing my writing.

Thank you to my family –
Jon, Josie & Jade Hocking, Carole & Brian Krempa, and Jenny & David Hocking.
Thank you to my 'guides' –
Hollie Bakerboljkovac, Jackie Barlow, Dr Brad Burgess, Stacey Casey,
Rebecca Ensign, Patricia Falcetta, Dr Paul Gooding, and Lisane Hurtubise.

I'd also like to thank you, the reader. Thank you for reading my poem, and for the connection that is made when we experience art that comes from a place of authenticity. I hope that you will find permission to love, accept, and have compassion for yourself – *monsters and all.*

ABOUT THE AUTHOR

Jamie Hocking is a former 'painfully shy, gifted kid' who eventually found that she is actually autistic with ADHD. Jamie began writing poetry in her early 20s. Although she never intended on becoming 'a poet', her emotions had to find some way out and poetry was their chosen path. Jamie has mostly kept her poetry to herself, but now in her mid-40s she's ready to let the world see the monster that she is — some of the time. The rest of the time, she's a dedicated wife, mother, and writer. Jamie provides an unflinching look at her life through her blog where she shares poetry, stories, and the life lessons that she's finally learning (and some she just keeps repeating) now that she is beginning to love the woman who was hidden behind the mask for too long.

www.jamiehocking.com

www.autismatmidlife.com

MONSTER
MERCHANDISE

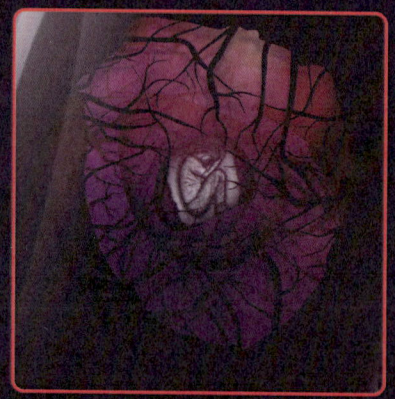

Designs subject to availability

CONSIDER SUPPORTING MY WORK BY PURCHASING MONSTER MERCHANDISE AT

WWW.JAMIEHOCKING.COM

Milton Keynes UK
Ingram Content Group UK Ltd.
UKRC031234101123
432324UK00001B/2